The European Union (EU) was formed to bring together the countries of Europe.

The EU helps its member countries with issues such as trade, security, and the rights of citizens. By 2013 the group had 28 member countries.

However, in 2016, one member—the United Kingdom—voted to leave the EU. The country officially left the union on January 31, 2020.

Today it is comprised of 27 member states.

European Union Map

Country: Austria
Capital: Vienna
Currency: Euro
Official language: German
EU member country since 1995, Euro area member since 1999, Schengen area member since 1997

Country: **Belgium**
Capital: **Brussels**
Currency: **Euro**
Official language: **French, Dutch, German**
EU member country since 1958, Euro area member since 1999, Schengen area member since 1995

Country: **Bulgaria**
Capital: **Sofia**
Currency: **Lev**
Official language: **Bulgarian**
EU member country since 2007

Country: **Croatia**
Capital: **Zagreb**
Currency: **Kuna**
Official language: **Croatian**
EU Member State since 2013

Country: Cyprus
Capital: Nicosia
Currency: Euro
Official language: Greek, Turkish
EU member country since 2004, Euro area member since 2008

Country: Czech Republic
Capital: Prague
Currency: Koruna
Official language: Czech
EU member country since 2004, Schengen area member since 2007

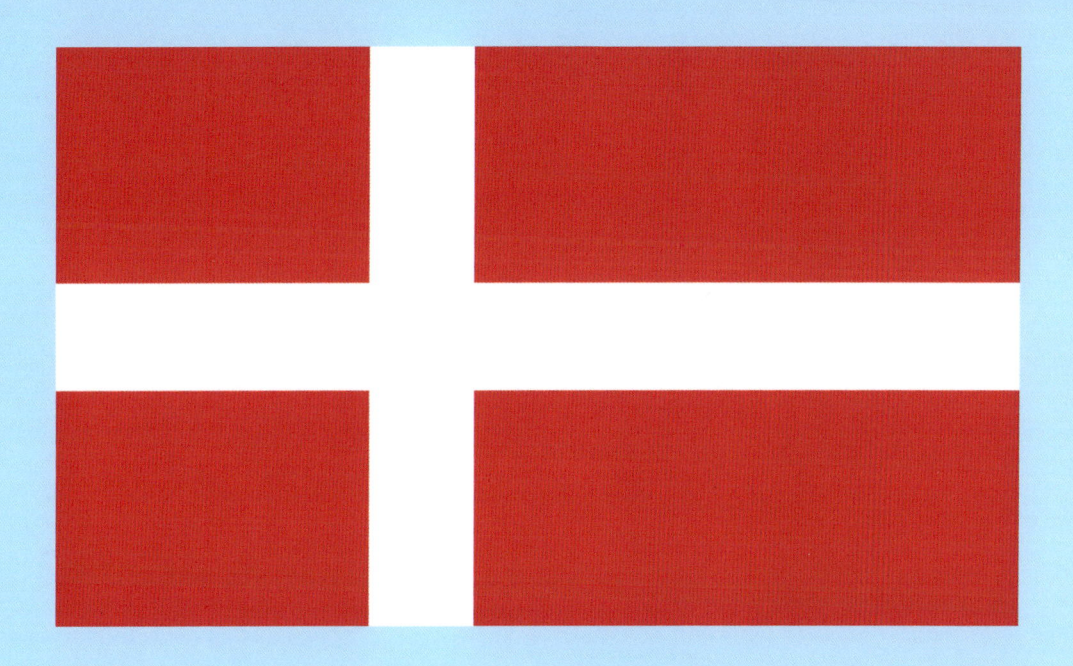

Country: Denmark
Capital: Copenhagen
Currency: Krone
Official language: Danish
EU member country since 1973, opt-out from euro, Schengen area member since 2001

Country: Estonia

Capital: Talinn

Currency: Euro

Official language: Estonian

EU member country since 2004, Euro area member since 2011, Schengen area member since 2007

Country: Finland
Capital: Helsinki
Currency: Euro
Official language: Finnish, Swedish
EU member country since 1995, Euro area member since 1999, Schengen area member since 2001

Country: **France**
Capital: **Paris**
Currency: **Euro**
Official language: **French**
EU member country since 1958, Euro area member since 1999, Schengen area member since 1995

Country: Germany
Capital: Berlin
Currency: Euro
Official language: German
EU member country since 1958, Euro area member since 1999, Schengen area member since 1995

Country: Greece
Capital: Athens
Currency: Euro
Official language: Greek
EU member country since 1981, Euro area member since 2001, Schengen area member since 2000

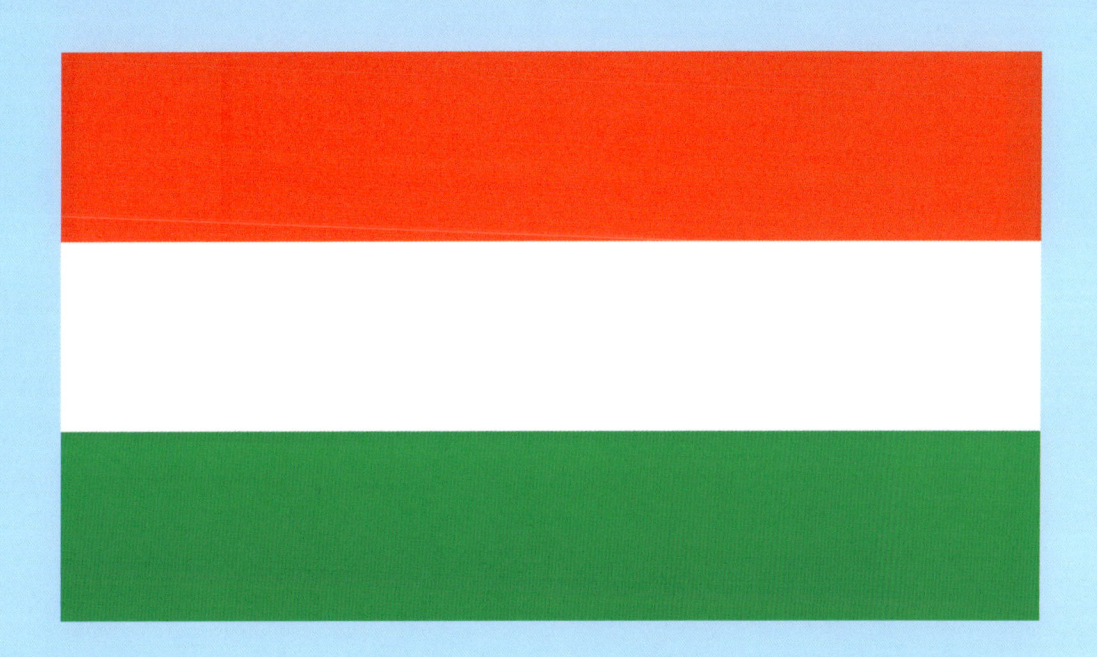

Country: **Hungary**
Capital: **Budapest**
Currency: **Forint**
Official language: **Hungarian**
EU member country since 2004, Schengen area member since 2007

Country: Ireland
Capital: Dublin
Currency: Euro
Official language: English, Irish
EU member country since 1973, Euro area member since 1999, opt-out from Schengen area

Country: Italy
Capital: Rome
Currency: Euro
Official language: Italian

EU member country since 1958, Euro area member since 1999, Schengen area member since 1997

Country: Latvia
Capital: Riga
Currency: Euro
Official language: Latvian
EU member country since 2004, Euro area member since 2014, Schengen area member since 2007

Country: **Lithuania**
Capital: **Vilnius**
Currency: **Euro**
Official language: **Lithuanian**
EU member country since 2004, Euro area member since 2015, Schengen area member since 2007

Country: **Luxembourg**
Capital: **Luxembourg**
Currency: **Euro**
Official language: **Luxembourgish, French, German**
EU member country since 1958, Euro area member since 1999, Schengen area member since 1995

Country: Malta
Capital: Valletta
Currency: Euro
Official language: Maltese, English
EU member country since 2004, Euro area member since 2008, Schengen area member since 2007

Country: **Netherlands**
Capital: **Amsterdam**
Currency: **Euro**
Official language: **Dutch**
EU member country since 1958, Euro area member since 1999, Schengen area member since 1995

Country: Poland
Capital: Warsaw
Currency: Zloty
Official language: Polish
EU member country since 2004, Schengen area member since 2007

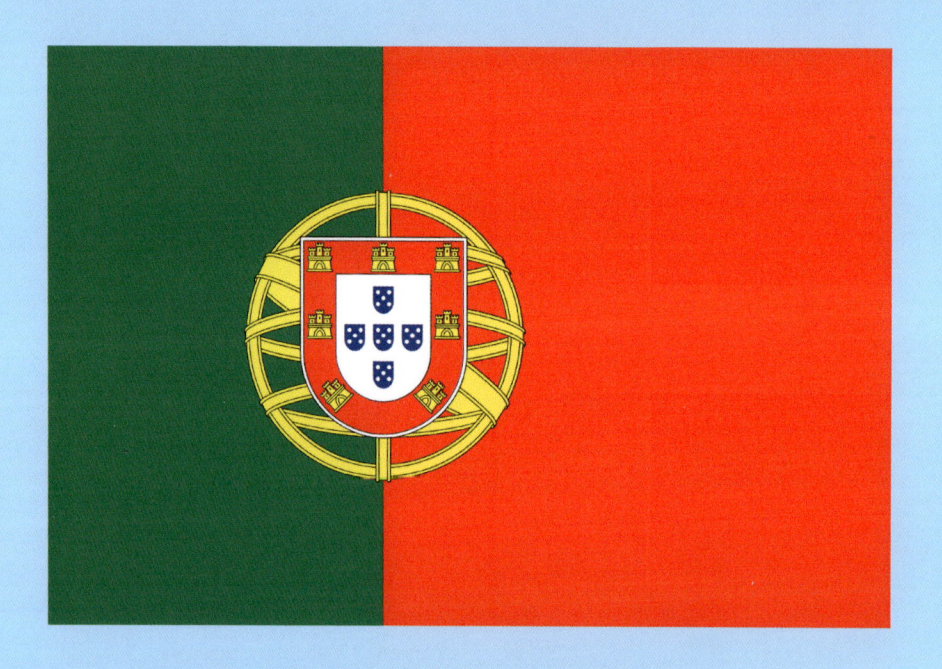

Country: Portugal
Capital: Lisbon
Currency: Euro
Official language: Portuguese

EU member country since 1986, Euro area member since 1999, Schengen area member since 1995

Country: Romania
Capital: Bucharest
Currency: Leu
Official language: Romanian
EU member country since 2007

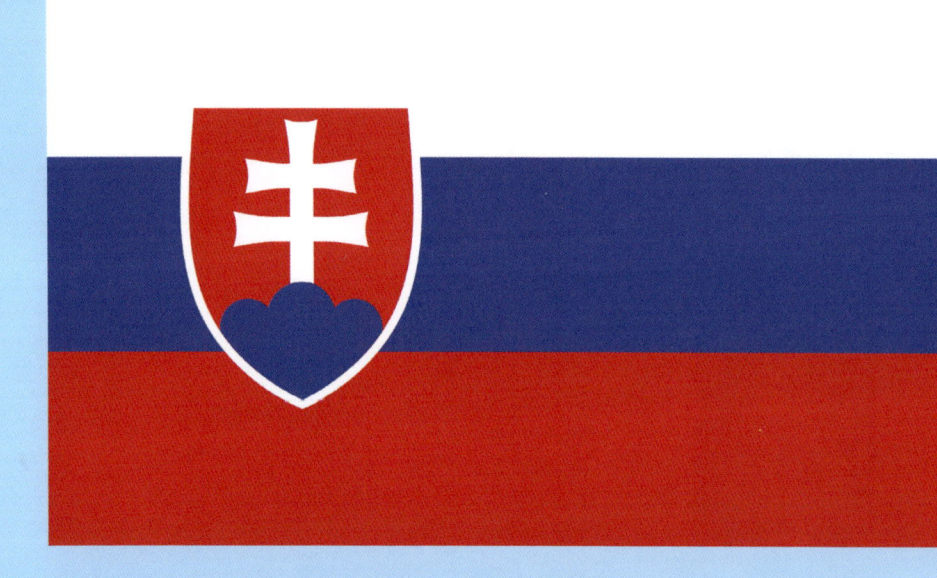

Country: Slovakia
Capital: Bratislava
Currency: Euro
Official language: Slovak
EU member country since 2004, Euro area member since 2009, Schengen area member since 2007

Country: **Slovenia**
Capital: **Ljubljana**
Currency: **Euro**
Official language: **Slovenian, English**
EU member country since 2004, Euro area member since 2007, Schengen area member since 2007

Country: **Spain**
Capital: **Madrid**
Currency: **Euro**
Official language: **Spanish**
EU member country since 1986, Euro area member since 1999, Schengen area member since 1995

Country: Sweden
Capital: Stockholm
Currency: Krona
Official language: Swedish
EU member country since 1995, Schengen area member since 2001

*

The flag has 12 stars because the number twelve is the symbol of completeness and unity.

*

The European anthem is "Ode to Joy" taken from the Ninth Symphony of the famous German composer and pianist Ludwig van Beethoven.

*

The Europe Day is celebrated on 9 May.

Created By

Tomasz Dabrowski

Source:

leadthecompetition.in

european-union.europa.eu

kids.britannica.com

en.wikipedia.org

Printed in Great Britain
by Amazon